W9-BDI-125

ALSO BY JILL BIALOSKY

The End of Desire

Wanting a Child
(coedited with Helen Schulman)

Subterranean

Subterranean

poems

JILL BIALOSKY

Alfred A. Knopf   New York   2001

THIS IS A BORZOI BOOK
PUBLISHED BY ALFRED A. KNOPF

Copyright © 2001 by Jill Bialosky

All rights reserved under International and Pan-American Copyright Conventions.

Published in the United States by Alfred A. Knopf, a division of Random House, Inc.,
New York, and simultaneously in Canada by Random House
of Canada Limited, Toronto.
Distributed by Random House, Inc., New York.

www.aaknopf.com

Knopf, Borzoi Books, and the colophon are
registered trademarks of Random House, Inc.

Library of Congress Cataloging-in-Publication Data
Bialosky, Jill.
Subterranean : poems / by Jill Bialosky.
p.   cm
ISBN 0-375-41314-6 (hardcover) — ISBN 0-375-70972-X (pbk.)
I. Title.
PS3552.I19 S84 2001
811'.54—dc21

2001033824

Manufactured in the United States of America
First Edition

For David and Lucas

While wandering in the well-tended gardens,
she had innocently picked a pomegranate
from a drooping branch, and had placed in her
mouth seven seeds taken from its pale husk.

—Ovid, *Metamorphoses*

CONTENTS

I

Subterranean   3
Flirtation   5
Terminal Tower   6

II

Torture   11
Interior with Child   21
Shadow Life   25
Four Versions of Rain   32

III

Mystery   39
The Wrath of the Gods   40
Music Lesson   42
The Fate of Persephone   44
The Circles, the Rings   48
The Adolescent Suicide   52
The Fall   54
Virgin Snow   56
A Dream of Winter   58
Raping the Nest   60
Temptation   61
Seven Seeds   63

IV

Landscape with Child   67
The Swan   68
A World Foregone Though Not Yet Ended   69
History of Longing   70
Oracle   71
A Child Banishes the Darkness   72
In Search of the Sublime   73
The Aviary   75
The Boy Beheld His Mother's Past   76
Thanksgiving Primer   77
The Barbecue   79
The Arborist's Lament   80
Atonement   81
Pumpkin Picking   83

Notes   85
Acknowledgments   85

I

Subterranean

She did not know when it would happen
or how it would overtake her
or whether she would allow herself.
All I know is that she could not take it anymore
lying day after day underneath the hollow tree, waiting,
consumed by a kind of fire,
wondering if there is a type of love
that saves us or whether there was more
to the world than the familiar paradise
of her mother's complicated and vivid garden.
She smelled nectar in the labored-over
chrysanthemum and amaryllis,
but could not taste it.
I know if it were a flower it would have bloomed
in the cumulus overhead
void of volition and sin,
translucent as the filmy underside of a leaf.
If it were an animal she would have followed it,
but it was amorphous as feeling, weightless as dust,
turbulent as an entire undisclosed universe
radiating from the inner core beneath the earth
and, still, she longed for it.
Restless, she wandered from the elm
to the school-yard to smother an intensity
she could not squelch or simmer.
The wind swooned. Cement cracked. Deep into the underbelly
light traveled, no one in sight but his immense shadow,
and then a figure appeared out of the imagined dream
and matched it. So powerful, not for who he was
but for how her mind had magnified him
like a bug underneath cool glass,

every antenna and tentacle aquiver.
No sign of where she had been
or who she came from. Only knowledge
that it would never be re-created
except by this: putting words down on a page
and that she had forever compromised
the joy of summer for a dismal, endless winter.
And as the field of force gathered,
raping every last silvery bough,
tantalizing each limb,
she forgot *even* the feel of herself.
When it was over she felt moisture. Rain.

Flirtation

On the shocking-pink shag carpet we lit incense, smoked joints,
read passages aloud from Nietzsche and Kierkegaard, just to see
how far we could go. We conducted séances,
moved our hands along the pilot of the Ouija board, invited
    our boyfriends up
for sex, took acid, experimented with mushrooms, got stoned on
    Quaaludes.
My first friend shot herself with a pistol. Seared
in my brain is her blue-and-white-gingham dress, knock knees
and ankle socks trimmed with a neat border of lace from our first
    grade class picture.
We played Barbies underneath the dim alcove
in her room while her mother, paralyzed from a stroke, traversed
    the downstairs
in her wheelchair, Maraschino cherries floating in a Manhattan
    cocktail on her tray,
chain-smoking. When we pulled ourselves away from the complex
    drama
in Barbie's Dream House and walked down the staircase
there was a fog so thick in the room we could barely see her.
Why Jeannie and not me? Why her and not Nancy or Ava
or Joanie or Jessica? Why *her* and not you, dear reader? The one
    who mastered
the flirtation, the dead girl, she is the person
I remember when I long to travel further,
to see underneath.

Terminal Tower

From the top of the tower when the sun set in the Cuyahoga's brown
    waters
(the river that caught fire and made our city the laughing stock of a
    nation)
it cast a dark shadow over the industrial sky.
To the Van Sweringen brothers it was like the Eiffel Tower of Paris
conceived in 1925 like a favorite child in a family—it foreshadowed
Rockefeller Center and gave to our city the second-tallest building—
to us it was grand as Mount Olympus.
It was the place we imagined Zeus and his cronies conducted
their mortal business. There is a legend about a lost daughter
and a mother who must bargain for her return. Weren't we all lost
inside our daydreams and imaginings?
Didn't all of us who lived off the shores of Lake Erie want to be
    claimed?
On an overcast day you can still make out the intricate masonry of its
    patrician face.
It was where the fathers of our community worked, riding the rapid
    transit
from the safe suburbs through the poverty of the ghetto into the
    underbelly
of downtown. When we looked from the ground to the top of the
    tower
we felt our spirits elevate. Then I heard it, inside the crowds, the
    honking
of automobiles and shriek of an ambulance, the singular cry,
and he was there in all his omnipotence and I knew my fate was locked
inside the mortar of his mercurial façade like wet leaves pressed
into a mosaic on the pavement. In synagogue we learned
about Moses climbing the mount and God's deliverance
of the commandments. Whether the sound came from a wounded gull

or a school of dirty pigeons did not matter. Whether it was Zeus or
    God
the Almighty or my own vision of my lost father was irrelevant.
It was the idea of being greater than myself I coveted. It *was* terminal,
the longing. It *was* magnificent, a tower that did not look desolate
in its setting, a structure to provide an anchor to the observer's glance,
    a relief from the flatness of the world around us.
In the tower's square men clad in overcoats carrying briefcases
trafficked the street, rode its fifty-two floors to politick. And it was at
    the very top
where Zeus might have bargained with the prince of the underworld
for his daughter's return. As I looked up the sweep of the tower's
    long elegance,
I saw through a mass of smog that I might lose myself forever or I
    might survive.
I saw that he was looking after me, but that he was also indifferent.
I saw that love was fickle and adulterous and still I longed for him.
I saw that he betrayed us and that he could not save me.
I saw through the stone into the abyss. It was dark and splendid.

II

The daughter I bore, a sweet offshoot noble in form—
I heard her voice throbbing through the barren air
as if she were suffering violence. . . .

—"Homeric Hymn to Demeter"

Torture

I

It was very cold
the long walks
we took.

The orange glow
of a fire in a window,
yellow gourds on a table;

red flames of those
autumn leaves
spiking the streets

with color.
We walked.
We walked.

What else was there
but our walks.
One foot

in front
of the other.

II

Mice inhabited
our walls,
we heard them

scratching at night
and the sound
of their little feet

running from one wall
to another.
Rarely did they make

their presence known
beyond the walls
though once

on bed rest
with my first child
two mice slipped

between the splinter
of light
underneath the door

and the floor in the closet
where we stored
our wool coats

and ancient
vacuum cleaner
and dashed

across the floor.
A fear
I harbored

all those months
looked me square
in the eyes.

III

Our upstairs
neighbors are wrapped
in that cocoon

a baby brings
into a house.
No one enters.

No one gets
between them,
warmth drifts

down to us,
seeps
into the cracks.

IV

To stave off
loneliness
I took in two cats

for the company
not knowing
the female

was expecting.
I was in love
with a man

who lived
with another
woman.

He came to me
only in daylight
in the hours

between
my waitressing
shifts.

The steel sky,
cold, mercurial.
From my window

I saw the shame
in his face
as he walked up

the back
staircase,
watched

the shade
fall over it
when he turned

the lock
to my door
leaving

one woman,
entering the house
of another.

While we made love
in my twin bed
we could hear

the mother cat
turn in the drawer
where she had gone

to give birth.
The sound,
it was agony.

The flip-flops,
the thud,
thud, thud.

One she turned
her back on.
Why was the kitten sick?

Why did she refuse
to nurse it?
Was her death

preordained?
After we buried
her still wet

from the after-
birth,
and not the nurturing

rough tongue
of her mother,
a black, wet thing

no larger
than the palm
of my hand,

he came for me
but the sound
of his footsteps

on the warped
wood step
were weightless.

The sky vacant
of light
by then.

It was winter.
The Formica counters
cold.

My sheets,
the unsanded floors,
unbearably cold.

V

Another's
happiness
quiets me.

The image
of our neighbor
so tired from in-

terrupted sleep,
every day wired
she forgets

to change
her clothes,
wash her hair.

Day bleeds
into night,
light

bleeds
into the carpet.

VI

I had no stomach
for the traps
the super set

in our closet,
the kind with glue
where a mouse

would step into it
for a rectangle of cheese.
I couldn't bear

that kind of torture.

VII

Afterwards, the dry cleaner,
the Korean greengrocer,
the place

we went for croissants,
were forbidding
without the child

I had already
ingratiated
inside the white

space of my future,
already a mother
snaring her child

against her will.

VIII

That winter
was like one long
night.

I curled
against the wall
beside the bed

and turned
inward.
By then

there was no baby
to bring home
and we could no longer

live in the place
she was conceived.
The white walls.

The window seat
I lay in
from two to three

o'clock each day
for that sliver
of sun—

by April
we were gone.
It can happen.

When I hear
our neighbor's
footsteps

walking
back and forth
above us

to calm the colic
I remember
the window seat.

It is burned
there
in that slab

of light.
Behind
our walls,

I felt life move.

Interior with Child

I

I walked
the erratic
jumble

of streets
in the middle
of the afternoon,

still a refuge
from my life,
and ducked

into a museum
to see it,
the grief

and mourning
art is wrought
from.

II

The children
followed.
One bruised

her knee,
another cried
out.

Tripped.
They walked
into the Renaissance

rooms
like a line
of quiet

civilized
soldiers.
You could hear

the sighing
of their sneakers
on the stone floors.

III

A girl
not unlike
the image

I formulated
of my own
daughter

reached down
to pull up
her knee socks

bunched
at her ankles.
A boy shot

a rubber band.
In the silent
corridors

connecting
one gallery
to the other

they giggled.
In their eyes
burned

the desire
to flee
the stale,

trapped air
and enter
the living

breathing
park they glimpsed
through glass.

IV

In the still world
filled
with porcelain

statues,
girls with pearl
earrings

and shuttlecock
and details
of the Virgin

and Child
painted in gold,
I heard a child

call out.
It was August.
Out our brownstone

window
the morning
glories—

their petals
closing at dusk
like the lips

of a child
over her mother's
breast—

climbed
the soot-dirt
walls.

Shadow Life

I

In that quick-
silver
of time

between sleep
and waking,
the pitter-

patter
of footsteps
like rain

against a roof
penetrates
the membrane

of our dreams.
Half asleep,
the gravity

of a child's
body
presses up

against mine.
The stars outside
dissolve.

II

I studied
by day
and at night

gathered my
tips
in the pocket

of my waitress
apron
and shared my bed

with a boy
who later
went mad.

In the blue-gray
of that winter
conceived

on the rumpled
sheets of our bed
or in the midst

of dream
there was a child
between us,

the embryonic
nut floating
lost and unattached.

III

In the window-
less cellar
we touched

but never once
spoke
of what in-

extricably
bound us
like winter's

shadow.
All those nights
we held

each other
to keep
from floating

adrift,
lit
a candle

in the pitch
black,
and waited

until the moon
completed
its inevitable

course
and the candle
burned itself out.

IV

Surely the daffodils
have begun
to show

their yellow
crowns,
lifted,

a white frost
like a sheet
over the lawn,

the whirling
crescents
from the mobile

colliding
with the shadow
life in a boy's

room
when hot
with fever

he calls out
and doesn't
know me.

V

The snow
is wet
like rain.

It will not
stick
or accumulate

snuffing
out the color
like the winter

the snow
fell so heavy
and uncompromising

I barely made it
to work,
the light

so oppressive
I craved
the crush

of darkness,
the return
to the mildewed

and damp
underworld
already let

to strangers.

VI

As he tromps
through
snow

up to his boot tops
to fetch
some twigs

for arms,
I remember
winter's

triumph:
shock
of newly fallen

snow
burning
into the ground

like memory,
his insistent
pair of tracks

from one side
of the yard
to the other,

the blinding
translucent
face

of a boy
carving out
holes

so the snow-
man
we've built

can see.

Four Versions of Rain

I

Sky
half-mast,
gray,

long winter
dragging,
ground broken,

birds barely
awake.
The leaves

in shatters.
An evergreen
pulled up

from its roots
un-
tethered

blows
this way
and that

across
the field.

II

Underneath
the dim light
of the library

carrel,
the rain
battering

its frail
apology
against the window,

I remember
the boy
I knew

just out
of childhood.
Not a hint

of sun
on the naked
hill. Only

grass, shrub.
Face-to-face
in the waiting room

I wondered
where he had gone,
that boy,

would I find
him again?
On the hospital

bed
on top
of those white

stark sheets
I once
held him.

III

She is by
the windowsill,
the side

of a shingled house,
stubbornly
carrying a bucket

of sand,
a figment
more alive

than the rain
softening
the newly

sodded grass.
Rain stops.
Starts again.

Mud slips
and slides.

IV

After
the torrential
downpour

the sky
impartial
to the emerging

light,
I hear them
talking

in the kitchen,
the tink, tink,
tink

of their silver
spoons
against porcelain,

my son's teeth
crunching
his Cheerios,

and listen
(the rain
now a drizzle).

When I bend
down to tie
his shoe—

his first pair
embalmed
in bronze—

I think,
don't hold on
so tight,

let him go.

III

Pluto saw her, and loved her, and bore her
off—so swift is love.

—Ovid, *Metamorphoses*

Mystery

Out of darkness came chaos
and from chaos there was a child.
A daughter.
Hair the color of wheat and tarnish.
There was a great bed
like a calm lake you wanted to float along
on your back all day
and dream of a world untouched
by discord and violence.
A world entirely whole and sane
and unlacking,
where above in the mysterious sky
you could chart order in the stars
and constellations.
It was a mother's bed,
no less, and at night the child in her own
pictured the world her mother entered
after the bath had been drawn,
the last light extinguished,
when she returned to her cool sheets.
She imagined the surface sleek and frozen
like a thick layer
of ice
a child might scratch her skates on
and, underneath it, brooding and forbidding waters
and then the ice cracked,
heaven and earth divided
and her mother fell into open arms.
And when dawn came she'd had enough.
There was quiet.
There was no weeping.

The Wrath of the Gods

She walked to the back
of the hot bus, queasy from the smell
of gasoline, past the place where boys congregated,
checking out each girl who dared to pass
the unspoken initiation
to the tiny bathroom
suffocating as a confessional
to discover for the first time its dark stain.
After the raucous pounding (the boys beating on the door)
quieted, she emerged into the dim light
but nothing had changed.
No boy later that night slipped into the empty seat
to whisper in her ear.
No girls flocked around her to share
in the newfound glory.
If there were gods, they were sent here
for one purpose, to decree that out of abundance
was pain, and from suffering
perhaps one day a child.
At the top of the monument
that brought them on the journey
early that day, tired after their triumph
(eight hundred and ninety-seven stone steps!),
she knew she was at the edge
of something grand and momentous
where she could see the glimmer—
the Lincoln and Thomas Jefferson Memorials
and our nation's Capitol, the dotted figures
of lovers strolling in the park,
the cherry trees in blossom!—
of what lay beyond

the guarded, serpentine walls
of her suburban community
where she might one day
forge her independence.
On the mount she could feel the press
of sun anointing her face, the air
like joy, building inside her;
the presence of our founding fathers
no longer imposed its dense weight.
But it wasn't until her mother picked her up
at the high school in the twilight
after the journey
that she knew no one
(perhaps not even the gods)
was watching.
The stars trembled.
The restless moths went at the streetlamp.
In the yard crickets screeched.
Twigs snapped.
The red, poisonous berries
from the tree shading her driveway
shed on the windshield of their car.

Music Lesson

I thought I was like her.
I would have sung, played the violin, piano, flute,
made music my life's work. I could hear the rapture;
the sound of the metronome as we stood straight,
chin up, heels of our Mary Janes
and loafers against the wood step.
Sometimes on the way to school,
I felt a melody build in the cave
of my body like a sudden
brightness just before letting go.
In assembly we stood in tiers depending
on our height as if we were the chorus
on the steps of the Theatre of Dionysus
looking into the hollow stage
in anticipation of a great tragedy.
We followed the tempo
against the movement of our maestro's stick,
watched the O of her lips
as she mouthed the words. I concentrated.
I let the air fill my diaphragm
just as she instructed.
Once I looked away from her
and turned, just a quick glimpse, to look at him.
Like Narcissus, he would have found a pool,
a lake, his image in the glass of the music room's window
and looked at his reflection all day. Still,
like a love-struck nymph (I was only a child)
I liked to watch.
To feel the light brush of his breath
on the back of my neck as he sang.
My country 'tis of thee

sweet land of liberty
of thee I sing;
land where our fathers died . . .
I sang louder, inhaling the air
and allowing it to sail through my being
until it was no longer me but the notes
of a beautiful bird dispatched
of her doom to echo the same notes
who had at last found her voice.
But it was too late.
In that one glance of betrayal
she saw inside the hidden chamber
my true self inhabited
and deemed to silence it.
My teacher looked at me
and put her index finger over her stern lips.
I never sang again. I was quiet.

The Fate of Persephone

I   The Vow

It is always winter.
The fields always
cold and brittle.

The barren trees
white as a shroud.
The night screams.

When I was full of her,
corn, wheat, fruits
of the orchard,

flourished. Now
I live without light.
I refuse to be

in the company
of the divine
without my daughter.

Wasted leaves
drown in the birdbath;
the statue in the garden

casts her eyes.

II   The Curse

Once she tore
the narcissus from the garden
(the shaft of sunlight

must have prematurely
drawn her gaze)
like a girl too eager

for love
she was plunged back
untethered

never to breathe again.
She kicked and screamed
but no one

(not even her mother
who raped the earth
in grief)

heard her nocturnal cries.

III   The Plot

They were brothers.
One lived for immortality
the other for seduction.

When the one who ruled
saw that his own daughter
was the token

of his brother's affection,
still he did not intervene,
or if he did,

it was with one caveat:
if she had tasted
the fruit,

she would bear
the curse
of her desire.

IV   The Fruit

The ancient black
cherry trees
and the graffiti

of their gnarled
limbs imprint
their shadow.

There at the juncture
of lawn and meadow
the crape myrtle bark

peels to a new
cinnamon color.
Still in the autumnal

haze,
the berry-berry
shrub,

still young, still vibrant
drops bright, violent
violet berries

as if in penance
for what the earth
must suffer.

The Circles, the Rings

I don't think it was snowing
the afternoon the child tied the long laces of her skates
together, hung them over her shoulder, and trudged
through the snow to the lake where they skated
so she would not be persuaded to roam
the forgotten plains lusting after boys,
committing unredeemable acts—self-flagellation,
starvation, promiscuity—tortured
by the blooming sense of brilliance
the flower of her youth had driven through her like a stake,
so that when she skated she was light
as a leaf blown toward the winds of heaven.

I don't think it was snowing
the late afternoon the child carved out
with her blades the nine rings and followed their course
as if lured from error, her scarf tangled
in her hair, so lost in the momentum of thrust and dig,
glide, glide, glide, that she dodged past other skaters without
   a glance.
The bodies of boys pushed into her, spun her, nearly slammed
her to the frozen ground, but still she skated on
crossing over into the shaded realm, further
into the subterranean depths as if in pursuit of a savior.

I don't think it was snowing
the moment she sensed there was no Beatrice
to lead her from folly, nor a guide as passionate or kind
as a poet to accompany her, and though she would have longed
to converse with Homer or Ovid, only the forest of incantations
from the Inferno unveiled their terrible fates.

Daylight turned to dusk and she skated in the dampness
consumed in a whirlwind as if confronted by the judge of the damned.
The hot dogs turned on the wheel, the sweet smell of hot chocolate
from the concession filled the gluttonous air,
a pair of skaters circled obsessively in the figure eight
as if entrapped in a state of limbo, but she skated on
transfixed by the dizzying power of her motion.

      I don't think it was snowing
when she took the third and fourth circles
past girls decked in furs and fancy hats, girls who were prettier,
smarter, craftier—how many hours had she daydreamed about
   their lives?
As they sped past, she saw the weakness of their eyes, the frailty
of their smiles, how their once beautiful bodies had gone to waste.
Around the fifth circle she swept past the clashing cacophony of boys
on their hockey skates, sticks in hand, warring against each other,
forsaking, now that the sun had fallen, the yellowness
of its eternal gaze.

      I don't think it was snowing
when the rebellious guards who stood watch
in front of the Iron Gates brought out the stretchers
and whipped past to help those who had fallen
and would not let her pass. It wasn't until the furies
descended and threatened to white out the landscape
that she heard the voice over the loudspeaker,
as if it were the messenger from heaven warning
the skaters to change direction, and watched the guards
carrying the mangled bodies of the children, that she recalled
how she once denied the dead immortality
and while the snow began to fall
she stood and prayed.

I don't think it was snowing
having minutes before blanketed the ice (it must have stopped)
when she circled the seventh ring, the ice choppy as rock
as she glided over the river of blood and nearly crashed
into two skaters stopped in a brawl and listened
to their angry accusations. She recalled the time she stole and lied,
the arguments with her sisters, how she forsook one friend for another,
the guilt she bore for surpassing the beauty of her mother.
If it were snowing it might have penetrated
the dried grass and broken roots,
it might have fallen like a wet rain onto her hair,
she might have been seduced
by its coppery glitter.

I don't think it was snowing
as she made the round of the seventh circle,
crossing one skate over the other, when she heard
in the air the chilling voices of the lost suicides
call out to her as if they were encased
in the triumphant branches of the trees
whose leaves were long ravished and winded.
In the forest beyond woodpeckers
went at the bodies of the trees; birds
shrieked and clamored.

I don't think it was snowing
as she glided around the circumference,
lost her footing and nearly fell onto the fragile patch of ice
where beneath the surface weeds, like serpents, coiled.
I don't think it was snowing when all those nights she was led
behind the ice rink's bleachers by one boy or another flashed
before her and she saw in the sky's dangerous transformations
the double-edged possibilities for how her past errors
might be reflected if she did not change course.

    I don't think it was snowing
when so lost in the thrust and *glide, glide, glide,* the noxious,
   delirious,
blinding rhythm, she reached the eighth circle. She skated faster,
past the apparition of the souls of the evil impersonators,
the souls of the counterfeiters, the souls
who bear false witness. She skated by all of those
who stood frozen and affixed by the transgressions
of the coldest wind until she reached the ninth circle
and her wonder was planted on the beautiful lone skater
in the middle, wearing a cloak dark as Satan.

    I don't think it was snowing
as the skater began the triple axel, his cloak fanned out
like black wings, three distinct but silent faces
flashed at her in turn, and though she desired nothing more
than his deep gaze burning into the curves and valleys
of the forbidden, a sudden gust, like a gentle hand,
took her in its arms, lifted her from the center of gravity,
and thrust her spinning (into the twilight) across the frozen lake.

The Adolescent Suicide

    I think
she knew the day she rode
the rapid transit downtown
to meet her great-aunt for lunch.
She must have walked,
jean jacket tied around her waist,
blond hair bleached
by the sun, past the local Chinese restaurant, a pub,
rubbing her free hand along the slab of a building,
ear turned to hear, the way a small boy puts his palm
to the tracks to feel the vibrations
of an oncoming train before crossing
to the other side.

    Metallic,
industrial sky, between concrete slabs
the crocuses push though.
Past the Terminal Tower, the arcade,
the Euclid mall, kicking through a mass
of city pigeons. Overhead
the buds held back
on the depressed,
twisted trees.

    The afternoon
the great-aunt took the girl to lunch,
her eyes were like a tree
without force, a sky without color,
a story without a legend.
I can just imagine it,
the girl at the table,

sorrow-less, clear, and cognizant,
the choice having already been made.
For once, her mind un-
encumbered by complication,
deliberate, without appetite.
To please her great-aunt,
the beloved orders her last meal:
A turkey sandwich. Pickle on the side. Diet Coke.

The Fall

Hollow, gargantuan gym, yellow wood floors polished slick
as a bowling lane where during the week boys in damp T-shirts

ran their laps, wrestled, kicked ass, on Saturday afternoons
was the private sanctuary where we slipped on our white gloves

and black leotards, fled the trapped air of our mothers'
station wagons for finishing school. Beneath the vapor

of ammonia the boys' gym still reeked of their sweat and hormones.
But as the autumn leaves held fast to the fertile maples and oaks

that regaled our suburban block, it was the girls who empirically
    reigned.
Self-possessed, confident, she turned on the phonograph,

diagonally moved across the room: she was nearly airborne.
Suck in your abdomen. Imagine a string holding your head high.

Sixteen girls fell into line. Was there any talk among us?
If so, no one remembers it. Only the exposed pipes on the ceiling,

the cling clang of the enormous furnace, as the descent began.
When we left the coterie of girls, and the padded, protected walls,

entered the thaw of those fall nights, led almost blindfolded
into the eerie cavern of the backseat of a boy's car,

there was no spring. No summer. No golden chariot.
Even the moon, changed forever, was abducted into darkness.

The wind, like a slap in one long swoop, stripped
the trees naked. Desire was indistinguishable from suffering,

from thought, from all that we had understood.
And yet, all those years in private under the cool quilts

of our beds, or in the cluttered attics of our minds, we craved it,
this terrible reckoning, where free of constraint, cleansed of regret,

we stepped out of ourselves, discarded our fears like clothing,
and entered the gate where love lived whole and breathing,

capable of both pain and beauty. It was all this we ever wanted
offered up like a shiny pomegranate: his breath on our neck,

his sex still governing the room, without our knowing it,
even when the last whistle had been long blown,

the last boy showered, locker slammed, lock turned,
long after the last boy had begun the endless walk home.

Virgin Snow

It happened, not as we had hoped,
underneath the stars, or along the banks
of a lake, or in an empty pasture,
but shut in amidst a virgin
snowstorm. It was among the coats and castoffs
on the bed in one of our parents' bedrooms,
they having vacated the premises for some exotic island
just, we naively imagined, so we might have our tryst.
The sensation, if I had to describe it,
was like stepping over the edge
of a cliff into water and not quite knowing
how deep the fall or whether we'd surface again.
I wish I could say it was sublime,
but here is what I remember:
the smoke and liquor like a halo
over the room, the scratch
of his rough jeans on my thighs,
the parting, swift as an axe
splitting wood in half.
Downstairs the party in full
motion as if Bacchus himself
were hosting the celebration
fully aware,
as the ball dropped
to announce the beginning of the new year,
and sailed down the long tunnel of Eros,
of what temptation would lead to.
There were no bells,
no feelings of enlightenment.
Later when I was alone in my bed

I thought one thing: What if it was true,
that in the end *he* was irrelevant?
I waited all night but not once did I hear
the nightingale fill the sky with reason,
or glimpse the sun muscle through the sky
to announce the birth of the miraculous.

A Dream of Winter

The sky weeps
like Persephone released

from the underworld
to favor us with flowers.

I am half awake
and if I close my eyes

I will be gone again.
Who are you

who are so close
in dream?

The ground with all this wetness
sinks beneath my feet,

so much desire
behind me

I must have dreamt away
an entire lifetime.

It is so hot we imagine
we'll never endure

such heat—these summer storms,
these brief flashes

of lightning, promise
a coolness long since bargained for.

Sleepless for want of you,
but if I take your hand

I disappear.

Raping the Nest

We found the blue small eggs inside the intricate nests
painstakingly made of twigs, hair, and down,

powerfully held them in the palms of our hands
like something fragile we might crush.

We were young, bored girls stealing eggs from a robin's nest.
I held one egg and shook it. There was a viable

tight little knot of life hot inside.
I wanted to crack it open to see what made it beat

so wildly in my hand. Above us in the sharp
summer air flocks swooped down making V's in the sky.

The days blended carelessly into one another
but, on this afternoon, because there was a boy I desired,

I did not care what would live or die or one day
fly into the air like the soul released from the body.

In the outline of the farthest branches I imagined his hand
on my face, the long complicated veins on his arms.

Temptation

Day was nearly breaking when we awoke.
The winter storm was abating.
It was the first day of creation.
I did not care that we had no money.
That what was between us was still as fragile
as the sheer of our curtains.
We had returned from Italy.
The image of Christ's hand
raised in blessing, the face of the Virgin
suffused with light, the naked
Child was in my head.
I thought of the divine foreknowledge
that lies behind her strange smile
and I wanted it.
Last night's storm hit so hard
the tree had fallen, exposing
the writhing roots, the marks
like scratches where it had hit on its bark.
I ached for something greater
to take possession
like sap in the belly
of the tree
necessary
to go on living.
The entire city was snowbound.
Ice formed intricate crevices
along our window. The trees
along the tree-lawn
except for the one sacrificed
by the storm were bathed in robes of white.
In the harsh light of that evening

like the force of two celestial planets
colliding into one, I felt it take hold.
I pictured the fresco, the gold light
circling her head. The stab
so severe it sliced into the center
of my being. When we peered
out the window the scene before us
was no less serene or benevolent
than the nativity: the shadow
of the tree's icy arms spread out
like an angel's in the snow, the lip of light
cresting, the quickening of day upon us.
Through the reflection of our breath on the cold glass
I saw your round Italian features
distilled in the clairvoyant image
of the child. The wind picked up,
leaving no evidence
of how it might enlighten
or harm.

Seven Seeds

I have been inside the third-floor walk-up
for months, like a bird confined to her nest.
I watch the sun press against the window
and filter through the veins and arteries
on the leaves of the cherry tree
in the little garden, the honeysuckle fading,
the vines slowly perishing.
                              By now
she will have sprouted
fine downy hair. Fingernails. Inhaled fluid
in the fetal lungs. I have witnessed
the slant of sky at every hour
of the day. Winter passed.
Then spring. Now the world
is so bright.
                    For one small peek
I bargain my confinement.
As I begin the walk
down the two flights of stairs
I know what it must have been like,
to see the fruit held out,
to know that soon she would be brought
back to her mother's warm-bedded
meadow and released
from the underworld.
                         Without foreknowledge
of her doom, she must have said to herself,
Just one seed,
and then tasted it,
and then another,
until she had consumed all seven,

the juice staining her lips crimson.
The light *was* bright that day.
It is shut now in my brain
like the star
made of seeds inside the flesh
of an apple when it is cut
open and exposed to the elements.
Yesterday my child ignorant
of a mother's grief
took those seeds
and planted them in the garden.

IV

Landscape with Child

Here I am for once on the other side.
Let me tell you what it's like.
There is barely a ripple on the lake.
Rain, yes, but we crave it, the temperate sound of water
on glass, on the wooden beams of our roof
and the sound of trucks on the road beyond the farm
breaking the perfect silence.
Our child sleeps now mostly through the night,
and when he comes in our bed we don't mind.
The horses in the barn have all quieted,
allayed by having endured last evening's storm.
We wake to the riot of birds
and we have vowed that we will learn their names
and families. It won't do to say the red bird,
or the blue one.
It is the same with these trees:
white pine, spruce, hemlock.
Yesterday a deer and her fawn crept behind a stand of them,
the fawn nursed, and the deer watched ahead,
on the lookout for danger so they might not come to harm.
Still we live in fear, but it is this field
of black-eyed Susans and bleeding hearts,
not their beauty, but how well they live without us,
we have come to depend on.
The deer and her fawn did not linger.
They shot through the open field
to the brambles and brush on the other side.
Who knew what would become of them.
We have learned to spot chicory and a spray of lavender.

The Swan

No matter the hour
of night or day,
she's there—always
at one shaded bank
of the pond
or the other.
Always alone.
Once, it almost frightened me—
she was in the center,
not a ripple on the lake,
not her mate,
nor another wading bird in sight—
so regal and pure, and unharmed,
so unafraid, it seemed,
of solitude,
so sure.

Imagine, desire gone,
no longer essential.
Not touch, perhaps one luxury—
memory—to sustain her.

A World Foregone
Though Not Yet Ended

It is your small body on my white sheets
curled up beside me, pulling at my skin
as if you want to get back inside,
that keeps me up at night.
Yours is the face I awaken to.
I watch your body growing plump with milk
and know every new fold and mark.

At night I sit on the deck and watch
the stars unfold. There is little wind.
I have forgotten what it was like when the moths
pressed against the light. The vibrant color
of ripened berries.
The moan of an animal.
When he comes to me, half-filled glass
in his hand, wanting
me to touch him, I hear
you stir in your crib. I know what your body feels like.
The soft skin of a flower, not bruised, not yet
in torment. The wet crease at the back of your neck. All night I listen
for your wordless sounds.

History of Longing

On a clear day from the deck
you can make out on the horizon
the lip of ocean
and in the foreground
a spray of wildflowers and the fence
leading to the field where horses graze.
But what I love most is the moisture
of the sea in the air, the salt you would taste
on a child's skin if you were to kiss it,
and from one of the bedrooms
if you happen to wake up in the early dawn
out of fear you remember from childhood
and thought long since gone—
before you understood that love
is immortal—
you would see the iron dawn
break against the window
and hear the rise and fall
of sleepers' breaths in the other rooms.
And when morning had fully crested,
the sound of church bells.
From the road if you were to come up in the dark
you'd make out only the light on the porch
and the smoke rising from the chimney
like a signal from survivors of a wreck
but they would be strong enough to guide you.
But what if just like that it was gone,
the sky bereft
and the children hungry?

Oracle

There was a chill in the ocean air,

despite the momentary surge of sunlight through the dense clouds,

but they were by the sea—

the ominous swoon of black birds overhead beginning

their necessary migration

in that small division of time

when nothing more was expected than this: to be together by the sea.

Shouldn't the child run between his mother

and father without fear

and shouldn't she hold her husband's hand

and shouldn't he watch from a distance

as she chases their child on this barren

stretch of eroding beach and amidst the sound of gulls screeching,

stench of seaweed, whip and pull of the wind,

shouldn't they hear the sound of laughter

though already the shadow has been cast along the beach?

A Child Banishes the Darkness

The child presides over our lives like the
blinding presence of tall white pines. In the
low room she hovers; she is the dark un-
tamed place, like a thicket in a neglect-
ed wood where I fall to after each new
loss, the unforgotten dream buried like
a small toy under layers of frozen
un-raked leaves. She is the hidden secret
we don't talk about because there is noth-
ing left to say. So much snow on the roofs
of tall buildings, along the cobbled streets,
in the eaves, and on the narrow bridge and
in the quiet palm of the newborn trees.
Nothing left to fear. All the earth is calm.

In Search of the Sublime

How did she have the courage night after night to extend herself
high and blind as a suicide into the unknown to grasp an outstretched
   arm?

I fled the balcony where Uncle Joe, bedecked in his lodge brother's
   hat,
reserved seats for us each year (he died of Parkinson's) and circled
   down

the back stairs. Behind an open door they kissed like star-crossed
   lovers.
The strange heat of it, how it could move air, or sand, or dust.

She is in the center of the ring, the beam of light's sole focus.
Against the ominous timbre of the drum, the net drops.

Sequined, hair wrapped high in a jeweled tiara, leg held in arabesque,
forsaking tranquillity, in pursuit of reinvention, she flings

from one swing to another like an exotic, bedazzled bird
in search of the sublime. In one free-floating, heart-stopping

moment she is pawned off, like an undesired object, from one hand
to another. Deaf to the gasp-held hush, into the odor of damp hay

and illusion's grandeur, she looks straight into the eyes of immortality.
One slip of her lover's resin-coated foot off the rope, one beat
   out of time,

could kill her. We will all die, whether underneath a tent of stars, or locked in the car's exhaust, or in a hospital bed.

The weak sun collapsed through the cracks in the canvas exposed her caked-on makeup and ripped stockings; bleached-out costume;

her smile's gesture of despair—why hadn't I noticed before?— as she took her final bow.

The Aviary

Out of nowhere came the ravenous sound and I knew she had
   returned:
the pheasant escaped from the pheasant farm down the road:

wire, the cage of sun through the rafters, hay, dried corn, the smell
of dampness, the incubation of light. Patient hens perched

over their clutch of eggs, their eyes fierce, maternal;
heads bent as if in reverence to the fragility of the unborn.

Winter hardy, able to withstand bitter cold, plumage faded,
pecking her bill against our deck like a careless mother

no longer living in fear of dishonor, no longer ashamed,
abandoning her eggs to feast on scraps of our evening barbecue.

In the half-life of an interior room and the wilderness outdoors,
the papery-thin soul of one being and another, we hear her:

the sound of persistence against our wood echoing its desperate
acoustic, the leave-taking and the return. The horrible hatching.

The Boy Beheld His Mother's Past

The ivory wedding hat came tumbling down—
how long had it been stored away, untouched
like desire repressed and bound—
and fell to the floor with less than a hush.

How long had it been stored away, untouched?
The boy beheld his mother's past
as dusk descended with less than a hush.
Was it possible her marriage might not last?

The boy beheld his mother's past—
Who was she? Who else did she love?
Was it possible her marriage might not last?
Light abandoned the skylight above
and shadowed the rug where they once danced.

Was his life governed by fate or circumstance?
The curtains trembled without a sound.
On the rug where they once danced
the ivory wedding hat came tumbling down.

Thanksgiving Primer

The day I put my son's life in danger
even the fragile vase on the coffee table

was wiped free of dust, sparkling like the lights
around a nativity pasture at night, for our newborn's

first Thanksgiving. In the pale of morning,
unaware of tragedy or consequence,

still marveling that only six months ago
I had not known love to incarnate both

sorrow and happiness before I felt the grasp
of his small fingers, or the way the light

intensified when it cast its shadow in his room,
or the sound of a bird once I knew it would be the sound

he would hear, nor had I understood the necessity of milk,
the brilliance of knowledge, or ever prayed more

for the goodness of humanity, I turned my back
to my son teething on his plastic ring in the center of my bed

to baste the turkey. In an instant I heard the fall
on the wood floor, his piercing cry

containing all the pain and chaos of the universe.
After our blessings, platters of cranberries, sweet potatoes,

roasted turkey passed, I was still shaken.
How many times would I harm or put myself

before my son—and how would I know—
and like a child wrongly solving an equation

on the blackboard—the frail sound of chalk, its fallen ash—
what would be *my* punishment?

The Barbecue

On the plywood deck canopied by Connecticut trees
so tall and lush we felt dwarfed and insignificant,
the family gathered under green leaves.

There was barely a scratch of wind or breeze.
Someone lit the coals, poured the drinks
on the plywood deck canopied by Connecticut trees.

A boy hammered a swarm of bees.
One of us mourned her unborn child.
The family gathered under green leaves.

The humidity was like another child between
us we wanted to take inside and send to her room
above the plywood deck canopied by Connecticut trees.

The child who took a fall with bruised knees
would never find herself, the third we would lose to cancer.
The family gathered under green leaves
on the plywood deck canopied by Connecticut trees.

The Arborist's Lament

Tiny and red and rows and rows of them
like the eyes of the gods or the garnet
of a necklace. How they shimmer, how they
replenish like pure, unadulterat-
ed love. If I were an arborist in-
fatuated with trees, I'd sit under
the cage-like lattice of bark in winter,
a full-leafed skirt in spring to study their
twisted nature, it would be these tangled
vines climbing the mesh I'd most desire. Prune
and prune, and still more rows until the mind
is beside itself, full to the brim, in-
toxicated. Inside such soft membranes.
What more is there I don't yet understand?

Atonement

Along the bank
of the Hudson

in late September
the first day of the new year

we broke bread and threw it
into the river. Nine days later

from dusk to dusk
we do not eat. We thirst.

Early evening, a screen of light
behind the river. It is time

to forgive, to ask why
we still hold on.

Across the water
in that golden world

wildflowers fade,
shadow stains the grass,

the trees still regal
in their green armor

carry the weight
of a long history

of suffering
which in a month's time

will have let go.
We are weak from hunger

for love withheld
or unknown,

for what we've lost
and can never attain.

Even that small imperfect
flicker of light

is nearly extinguished.
High-pitched wail

of a lover's cry,
a deserted playground

in the distance.
Resolve crumbles

like the bricks and mortar
on our ancient temples.

Birds flock
and assail the sky

like a mass exodus.
The sun falls.

Pumpkin Picking

The day we take our son into the orange fields to go pumpkin picking,
he proudly wheels the wagon through the muddied rows

stopping now and then to observe the pumpkins,
how one is lopsided, another the shape of a woman's torso,

one the size of an October moon. Before us the gray, fractured sky
so close you feel you could walk into it and enter the other world,

the air the kind of cold you pray for by August.
By the side of the road a man is burning leaves,

the smell drifts through the tangled rows, seeps into our wool jackets,
    our hair,
the way loss penetrates every aspect of a landscape, from a frozen

patch of ground, to this stand of blue spruce in the distance.
While my son is strutting down one row, up another, filling his wagon
    with pumpkins,

occasionally kicking one that has broken loose and begun to mold,
I wander farther into the field through so many rows of orange heads

it's as if the souls of our lost children have entered this graveyard
where in a month's time the fields will be picked over, pumpkins splayed

open, smashed, left to rot. Ready to be pulped, seeds cleaned,
toasted, later carved into jack-o'-lanterns, these pumpkins haunt me.

How they grow wild, almost arbitrary, how they give so much
    meaning
to a boy. Look, their thick, husky umbilical stems wedding

them to the ground, how with a quick slice of a blade, even a hearty
    pull,
they are cast free from the earth toward heaven.

es, Book V, translated by Mary M.

to Demeter," author unknown, trans-

es, Book V, translated by Mary M. Innes.

IV: The Fruit," from "The Fate of Perse-
phone a_   article that appeared in the *New York Times
Magazine*.

The title of the poem "A Worl. Foregone Though Not Yet Ended" comes from
a line in Hart Crane's "Postscript."

Acknowledgments

Grateful acknowledgment is made to the editors of the following publications,
where the poems indicated first appeared:

Agni Review: "Subterranean"; *American Poetry Review:* "The Wrath of the Gods"
and "The Aviary"; *The Forward:* "Atonement" and also in *American Diaspora:
Poetry of Displacement* (University of Iowa Press); *Lyric:* "A Dream of Winter"
and "A World Foregone Though Not Yet Ended," originally titled "Hunger";
The Nation: "The Swan" and "The Barbecue"; *The New Republic:* "Temptation";
Open City: "Raping the Nest," "Landscape with Child," and "Virgin Snow";
Paris Review: "The Boy Beheld His Mother's Past"; *PN Review:* "History of
Longing" and "Mystery"; *Poetry:* "Seven Seeds"; *Sundog: The Southeast Review:*
"Torture" and "Shadowlife"; *Tin House:* "Pumpkin Picking"; "The Adolescent
Suicide" was first published in *Like Thunder: Poets Respond to Violence in America*
(University of Iowa Press).

*Special thanks to Deborah Garrison, Sarah Chalfant, Eavan Boland, Alice Fulton,
Harriet Levin, Lelia Ruckenstein, and Kate Sontag; and to the memory of Harry Ford
for his abiding faith.*

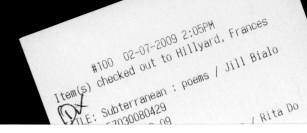

#100   02-07-2009 2:05PM
Item(s) checked out to Hillyard, Frances
TITLE: Subterranean : poems / Jill Bialo
57030080429
.09   / Rita Do

A Note About the Author

Jill Bialosky was born in Cleveland, Ohio. She studied at Ohio University and received a Master of Arts from Johns Hopkins University and a Master of Fine Arts from the University of Iowa. Her first book, *The End of Desire,* was published by Knopf in 1997. Her poems appear regularly in journals such as *Paris Review, American Poetry Review, Agni Review,* and *The New Republic.* She is the coeditor (with Helen Schulman) of an anthology entitled *Wanting a Child.* Bialosky is an editor at W. W. Norton and she teaches a poetry workshop at Columbia University; she lives in New York City with her husband and son.

A Note on the Type

Pierre Simon Fournier *le jeune,* who designed the type used in this book, was both an originator and a collector of types. His services to the art of printing were his design of letters, his creation of ornaments and initials, and his standardization of type sizes. His types are old style in character and sharply cut. In 1764 and 1766 he published his *Manuel typographique,* a treatise on the history of French types and printing, on typefounding in all its details, and on what many consider his most important contribution to typography—the measurement of type by the point system.

Composed by
NK Graphics,
Keene, New Hampshire

Printed and bound by
Edwards Brothers,
Ann Arbor, Michigan

Designed by
Soonyoung Kwon